South West C

NATIONAL

WALKS ALONG THE
SOUTH WEST COAST PATH

Ruth Luckhurst

PLYMOUTH TO FALMOUTH

A Coastal Publishing Limited Book

Editor Alison Moss
Design Jonathan Lewis
Production Peter Sills
South West Coast Path Project Manager Jo Kiddell

First published in 2013 by Coastal Publishing Limited
The Studio
Puddletown Road
Wareham
Dorset BH20 6AE

T: 01929 554195
E: enquiries@coastalpublishing.co.uk
www.coastalpublishing.co.uk

ISBN 978-1-907701-04-7

British Library Cataloguing-in-Publication Data
A catalogue record for this book is available from the British Library.

Printed and bound in Great Britain.

Front cover image: Rachel Papworth.

With great thanks to the South West Coast Path Team's partners, who help to maintain and manage the Coast Path, for providing pictures and contributing to the research for this book. In particular, we'd like to thank the Cornwall Area of Outstanding Natural Beauty (AONB), the National Trust and Natural England, as well as all the wonderful photographers who have supplied their pictures for use in this book.

Image Acknowledgements
(key: t:top, m:middle, b:bottom, l:left, r:right, c:centre)
Images in this book are copyright of the photographers and artists.

All Aerial photographs © Coastal Publishing Limited; Front Cover Rachel Papworth; Christian Browning 27m; Adrian Cooke 32t; Barry Lockwood 48b; Ruth Luckhurst 4m, 5b, 8b, 9m, 9b, 12t, 12b, 13tl, 16t, 16b, 17t, 17m, 17b, 20t, 20m, 21t, 26t, 27b, 32b, 37tl, 37tr, 40t, 41t, 44t, 45m, 49, 54t, 55t, 55m, 55b, 59m, 62t, 62b, 63m, 63b; Jessica McMullen 33t; Colin Milner 36t, 58t, 58b; National Trust 44m; Jennifer Rowlandson 48t, 59b; Roz Tabberer 13tr; Stuart Tormey 40b; Graham Woollven 13b.

CONTENTS

Introduction 4-5

Walks along the South West Coast Path

Plymouth to Falmouth

Walk 1 - Mount Edgcumbe to Kingsand 6-9

Walk 2 - Kingsand and Rame Head 10-13

Walk 3 - Looe, Talland and the Giant's Hedge 14-17

Walk 4 - Bodinnick, Polruan, Fowey 18-21

Walk 5 - St Catherine's Castle 22-23

Walk 6 - Lankelly and Menabilly 24-27

Walk 7 - Par Beach 28-29

Walk 8 - Black Head and Castle Gotha 30-33

Walk 9 - Mevagissey and Heligan Mill 34-37

Walk 10 - Portmellon 38-41

Walk 11 - Dodman Point 42-45

Walk 12 - Porthluney 46-49

Walk 13 - Tregenna 50-51

Walk 14 - Nare Head 52-55

Walk 15 - Gerrans Bay 56-59

Walk 16 - St Anthony Head 60-63

Safety and further information 64

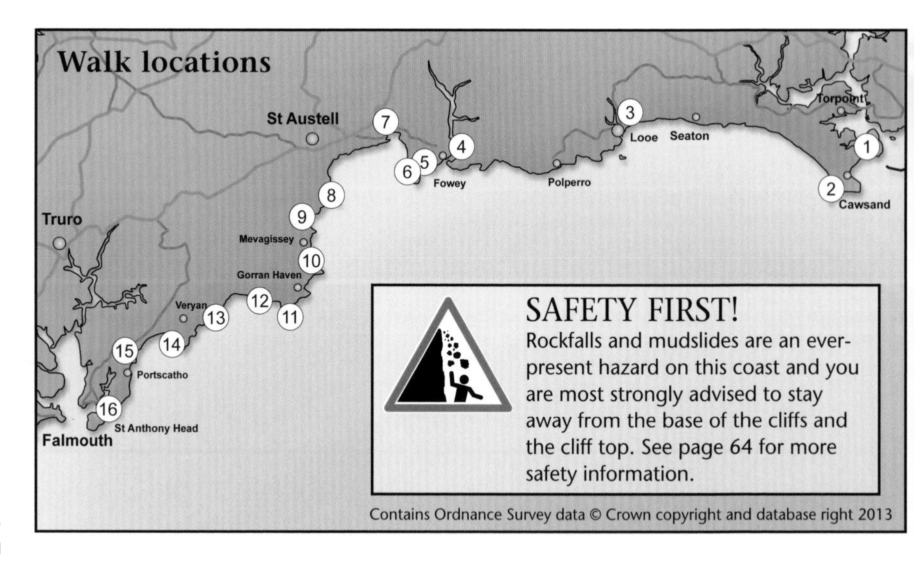

The sweep of land between the major waterways of Plymouth Sound and Carrick Roads is an unspoilt paradise of secret creeks, coves and tiny fishing villages. The South West Coast Path rises and falls between headlands topped with lighthouses, crosses and chapels, with wide-ranging vistas over land and sea, and turquoise waters lap on swathes of white sand on unspoilt beaches.

There are large areas of woodland, especially along the steep banks above the creeks around Fowey and Looe, and parts of them are very old, thanks to the historic practice of coppicing, which also makes them a haven for wildlife.

On a summer's day the grass beside the path is studded with wildflowers beneath banks of vivid gorse. Moths and butterflies whirl above, and bees hum in the bramble flowers where blackberries will grow and ripen in the autumn sun. Wildfowl and waterbirds abound, and colonies of seabirds nest on the cliffs. Occasionally seals can be seen offshore, and porpoises and dolphins

Plymouth Sound from Edgcumbe.

are regularly spotted in the River Fal, where the gaff-rigged ships of the Port of Truro Oyster Fishery belong to Europe's last commercial fleet powered wholly by sail.

But in winter, when the weather turns wicked, it becomes a remote place of gales and shipwrecks, where wild easterlies drive a heavy swell onto the shoreline, dashing the surf high into the air on the rocks below. Then you can see why the whitewashed cottages huddling in the lee of the headlands have shutters to close against the fierce winds.

It is an ancient land. Across the region, prehistoric people built themselves defensive forts and settlements to protect themselves from attackers arriving by sea. In the Dark Ages, drovers and traders and numerous Celtic saints and hermits passed through on their way from Ireland to Brittany. The countryside is crisscrossed with earthworks and bolstered with ramparts, and granite crosses mark paths, boundaries and burial sites.

It is a land of legend, too: many key figures of the Arthurian romances are said to have lived, died and been buried here.

Fishing was a way of life for many generations of coastal dwellers, and net lofts and fish cellars are a familiar sight in most villages, although nowadays the catch is mostly mackerel and lobsters. Around St Austell Bay are the remnants of the railway lines, quays and weirs which served the china clay industry and the tin mines.

Defence of the coastline, too, has left its mark on the land. Over many centuries, castles and blockhouses were built, strengthened and adapted as there were skirmishes with the French and Spanish, and these fortresses played their part in the English Civil War, too. Plymouth and Falmouth were major targets during two world wars and heavy artillery was brought in to defend both ports. Even the Cold War left its mark, in the form of a bunker near Veryan.

The quaint fishing village of Portloe has featured in many films and television series, and the Cornish writers A. L. Rowse and Arthur Quiller-Couch both lived here. Best-known of the area's literary celebrities was Daphne du Maurier, and many of her novels were set here.

Each of these sixteen short circular walks has been chosen to inspire and delight every walker, from the Sunday stroller to the dedicated enthusiast, and together they illustrate the many special features of this most romantic, hideaway part of the South West Coast Path.

Public Transport

Plymouth and Falmouth have good transport links to bus services and the main train lines to and from the county.

Most walks give information about the nearest car park. Information about public transport services for these walks can be found online at www.southwestcoastpath.com

The Traveline South West website provides up to date information about all public transport links.
Visit www.travelinesw.com
or call 0871 200 22 33.

Summer sun at Kingsand.

Kingsand
Friary
Manor
Lower
Anderton
Empacombe
P
Start/Finish
Mount Edgcumbe
Country Park
Fort
Picklecombe

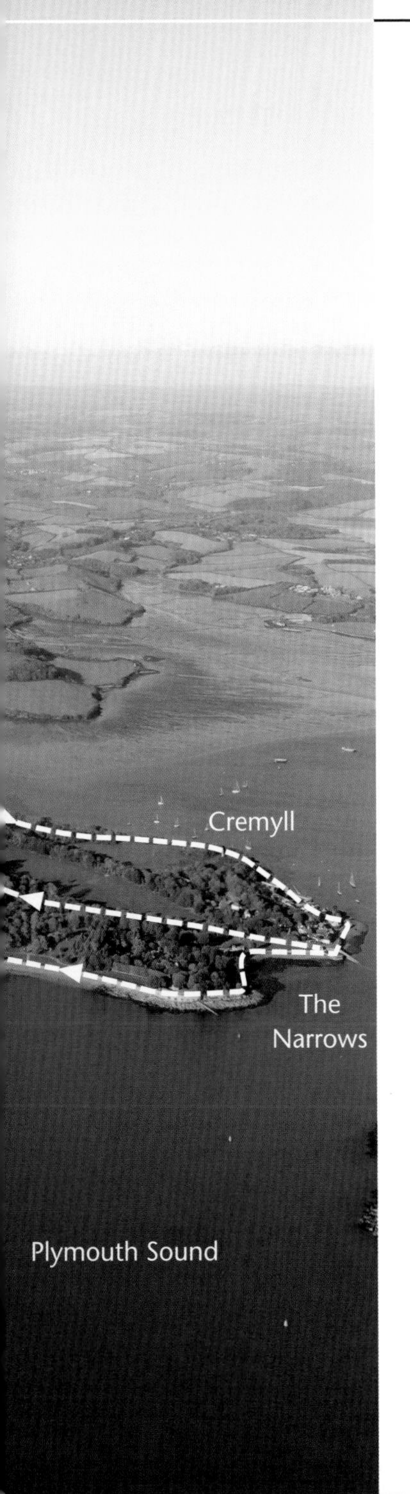

Walk 1 – Mount Edgcumbe to Kingsand

Distance	6 miles (9.75km)
Estimated time	3 hours
Difficulty	●●●●●
Ascent	981ft (299m)
Map	OS Explorer Map 107
Starting point	SX 446519

Notes: A fairly strenuous walk through the formal gardens, parkland and woods of Mount Edgcumbe, passing many features from its colourful history. There is a lot of ascent and descent, some of it steep, as well as steps and narrow paths that can be slippery in places.

From the car park by Maker Church walk back up the drive a short distance to pick up the path on the right, and follow it down to Lower Anderton, crossing the B3247 to go into the woods and continuing straight ahead when another path crosses yours shortly afterwards. Turn left for a short distance on the road at Lower Anderton and cross the road onto a path that leads around the riverbank to Empacombe. Follow the waymarkers and the directions posted at Empacombe to continue along the riverbank and come out on the path leading to Cremyll.

At the road, turn right then left, to go through the Cremyll Gate into Mount Edgcumbe. Stay with the path as it carries on around the headland through the park and into the woodland above Plymouth Sound. When the path appears to stop at a dead-end, take the sharp dog-leg to your right and climb the steps steeply uphill to join the South West Coast Path above The Narrows. Follow the acorn waymarkers for about 3 miles, bearing left to carry on along the shoreline every time the path forks.

Reaching the first houses at Kingsand, turn right onto the road and walk a short distance, to pick up the footpath to your right through the woods. Bear right in the woods to follow New Road out onto open parkland, staying on it as it veers sharply left to merge with Earl's Drive a little further on. Turn right here and pick up the footpath on your left to follow the field boundary and rejoin Earl's Drive beyond. Turn right and carry on ahead as a road joins from the left, to take the footpath on your right which leads past Friary Manor and then bears left along the hedge to return you to the drive to Maker Church and the car park.

Drake's Island was fortified to defend Drake's Channel, Plymouth Sound's only deepwater route into Devonport. It is linked to the Cornish mainland by a shallow reef known as 'The Bridge'.

From the eighth century the Saxons controlled both sides of the Tamar, and the parish of Maker (including Mount Edgcumbe) was a royal estate and remained part of Devon until 1844. The name 'Maker' comes from the Cornish word 'magor', meaning 'ruin'. Maker Church was built in 1186 and enlarged in the fifteenth century. It was the family church for the Edgcumbes, and the Earl's Drive, (originally known as 'The Terrace' and built in the eighteenth century), linked the church to Mount Edgcumbe House.

St Julian's Well, just below the church, is a tiny chapel and holy well, dating from the fifteenth century and restored in 1890.

Mount Edgcumbe was the home of the Earls of Mount Edgcumbe. Sir Piers Edgcumbe of Cotehele acquired the estate through marriage in 1493, and his descendant, Richard – a prominent politician – was created Baron of Edgcumbe in 1742. The third Baron was made the first Earl of Edgcumbe in 1789.

Empacombe.

The house is set in Grade I Cornish gardens, and the 865-acre grounds include no fewer than 55 Grade II or III listed features, many of which are visited during this walk. The grounds are open all year and admission is free to much of the estate, including the National Camellia Collection and the Orangery Restaurant.

The Orangery is in the Italian Garden, one of the earliest formal gardens here. Between 1750 and 1820, English and French Gardens were also created, while New Zealand and American Gardens were added in 1989, and a Jubilee Garden in 2003.

Near the Cremyll Gate is the historic Cremyll Ferry. This was first documented in 1204 but has been a major ferry crossing between Devon and Cornwall for more than a thousand years. The ferry ran between the twin settlements West and East Stonehouse, on either side of the Tamar.

A short distance on from the Orangery Restaurant is the Battery and Blockhouse. The Blockhouse is one of a pair of forts built by Henry VIII in 1545 to defend the mouth of the Tamar against French invaders. The Battery was built in 1747 as a saluting platform and was equipped with 21 guns with which to welcome visitors; but in 1863 it was rebuilt as part of Plymouth's defences. The Barn Pool, just beyond the Battery, is a sheltered deep anchorage that was used by the Vikings in 997.

A little way beyond Barn Pool is the Temple of Milton, a circular Ionic temple built in 1755 and inscribed with lines from Milton's Paradise Lost. Elsewhere, Thomson's Seat is a Doric pavilion bearing verses from James Thomson's The Seasons. Another seat, usefully placed at the top of the steepest section of ascent of this walk, is the Red Seat, also known as The Kiosk, a rest house once painted red. Built in the nineteenth century, this would have been handy for walkers who had braved The Zig-Zags – dramatic cliff-paths known at the time as 'The Horrors'. The lower parts of some of these paths have been lost in cliff falls.

The Picklecombe Seat, to the west, was constructed from a medieval doorway using carved stone from the churches of St George and St Lawrence at East Stonehouse. Below it is Fort Picklecombe, one of a ring of forts built by Lord Palmerston to defend Plymouth in the nineteenth century. None of the forts was ever used in war, other than as a deterrent, and for this reason they became known as the Palmerston Follies. Fort Picklecombe is now converted to holiday apartments.

Woodland path at Empacombe.

Well at Edgcumbe

Wringford
Farm
Kingsand
Wiggle
P
Trehill
Start/Finish
Wiggle
Cliff
Rame
Polhawn
Cove
Rame Head

Walk 2 – Kingsand and Rame Head

Distance	5.25 miles (8.5km)
Estimated time	2¾ hours
Difficulty	●●●●●
Ascent	847ft (258m)
Map	OS Explorer Map 107
Starting point	SX 431503

Notes: The frequent ascent and descent of this walk is amply rewarded by tremendous coastal views and many historical features. Take time to browse through the twin seventeenth-century fishing villages of Kingsand and Cawsand.

From Cawsand car park turn left onto St Andrew's Place and descend to the Square. Turn right onto Pier Lane to follow the South West Coast Path uphill and around Penlee Point. If you detour left at the grotto to Penlee Battery, retrace your steps to the Coast Path.

Carry on ahead to the chapel at Rame Head, turning right just before you reach the chapel, to drop to Polhawn Cove. Polhawn Fort, another Palmerston Folly, lies below the path as you descend.

Ignoring the paths uphill to Rame and Trehill, continue ahead along the Coast Path. Turn abruptly right with the Coast Path above Wiggle Cliff, past the car park, turning sharp left beyond then bearing right on the road towards Wiggle. Take the footpath on your right at the left-hand bend as you approach the buildings, coming out at Wringford Farm. Bear left and cross the road to continue on the footpath ahead, through the trees to New Road. Turn right here to return to the car park.

By the path, high above the sea at Penlee Point, is Queen Adelaide's Grotto. Originally a cave used in the eighteenth century as a watch house, the stone arch building was added after Princess Adelaide visited in 1827, four years before she was crowned Queen Consort. The Earl's Drive had been extended to here a few years before her visit.

Seaside chapel at Kingsand.

Below the grotto is Penlee Battery, a Victorian fort constructed in the late 1800s and used throughout both world wars. One of the earliest and largest guns sited here was hauled by 80 horses up specially constructed steps, taking two weeks to get here. The gun split its concrete bed on its first firing and was hastily replaced with six smaller guns. Penlee Battery is now a nature reserve and is famous among naturalists as the place for the first (and only) British sighting of the Green Darner dragonfly in 1998.

The chapel on Rame Head was built in the fourteenth century and dedicated to St Michael. It was first licensed for Mass in 1397 and is thought to have been built on the site of an earlier Celtic hermitage. In medieval times it doubled as a lighthouse, as did many of the chapels or hermitages built on the coast, with a light burning in a window overnight. It was from St Michael's Chapel that the Armada was first spotted.

There was also an Iron Age promontory fort on Rame Head, and there is an earthwork from it visible across the neck of the headland.

Polhawn Cove.

Queen Adelaide's Grotto.

St Michael's chapel on Rame Head.

Eddystone Lighthouse

Thirteen miles to the southwest of Plymouth is the famous Eddystone Lighthouse. It was the first lighthouse to be built on a small rock in the open sea, and stands on a reef of a garnetiferous gneiss, the only place in south west England where this rock type, famously associated with northwest Scotland, is to be found.

The current lighthouse is the fourth to stand on the Eddystone Rock. The first was built by Henry Winstanton after he lost two ships on the reef, and the Admiralty considered the project so important that they provided a warship to protect those involved in its construction, since England was at war with France at the time. The lighthouse was octagonal and survived its first winter in 1698 but needed major repairs, during which it became dodecagonal. The Great Storm of 1703 swept it away and it was replaced with a wooden tower built around a core of brick and concrete. This survived 46 years before it burned down.

Civil engineer Robert Smeaton modelled the third lighthouse on the shape of an oak tree, for strength, and built it of granite blocks, using pioneering techniques such as 'hydraulic lime', a concrete that would set underwater. This lighthouse withstood the elements for 118 years, before erosion of the rock made it unstable and it was dismantled. The top half was removed to Plymouth Hoe, where it still stands, while the stub remains on the rock, beside the fourth and current lighthouse, erected in 1882 and still in use.

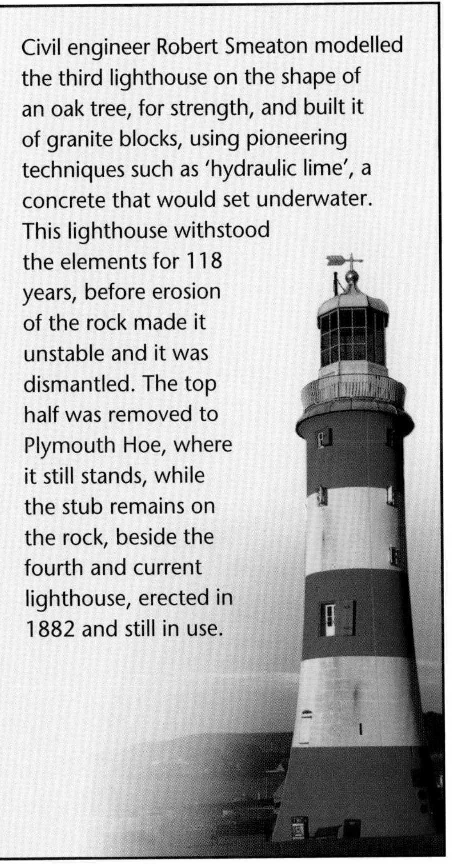

Watergate
Kilminorth
Looe
Parker's
Cross
Tencreek
Talland
Talland Bay

Walk 3 – Looe, Talland and the Giant's Hedge

Distance	7.25 miles (11.75km)
Estimated time	3½ hours
Difficulty	•••••
Ascent	1076ft (328m)
Map	OS Explorer Map 107
Starting point	SX 253537

Notes: A long walk with lots of ups and downs, some of them steep. This route travels through an ancient woodland, and takes in a major earthwork from the Dark Ages, as well as a Celtic chapel.

From Millpool car park in West Looe follow the riverbank westwards towards Watergate. Choose either route through the woods. At Watergate turn left onto the road and follow it uphill through Kilminorth, carrying on between the houses and round the sharp right-hand bend, to come out at Parker's Cross about ¾ mile later.

Crossing Polperro Road, continue ahead on the small road past Waylands Farm to Tencreek. At Tencreek Farm turn right onto the lane and walk downhill, turning left on the road at the bottom. Follow the road as it curves left, to pick up the South West Coast Path on your right.

Walk east with the Coast Path as it hugs the coast all the way to Hannafore, where it sweeps to the left down Marine Drive and travels alongside the harbour to Looe Bridge. Carry straight on past the bridge and drop downhill to return to Millpool.

According to local legend: 'Jack the Giant, having nothing to do, built a hedge from Lerryn to Looe.' Giant's Hedge is one of the largest ancient earth banks in the UK, stretching some 9 miles from the Fowey Estuary to Looe. In places it is up to 15 feet high and 24 feet wide, although the remnants visible in Kilminorth Woods are no higher than 3 or 4 feet. It can be seen along the upper path through the woods.

It is thought to date from the Dark Ages, and was probably the boundary of a tribal chief's petty kingdom (one of many small kingdoms around Britain before the tenth-century creation of the kingdom of England). An alternative theory is that it may have been a 'last-ditch' defence by the Cornish against the Saxon incursions of the ninth and tenth centuries.

The Guildhall in East Looe.

Kilminorth Woods is a local nature reserve and is a haven for wildlife. It is an ancient oak woodland that has been continuously wooded for more than 400 years. The practice of coppicing has prolonged the life of individual trees throughout the woods.

The banjo pier from East Looe.

Many species of birds nest here, including birds of prey such as the buzzard and peregrine, waterbirds such as herons and shelducks, and songbirds such as mistle thrushes and goldfinches. Spring flowers include primroses and bluebells, followed by dog violets and wood anemones, and many different species of moths and butterflies flutter through the woods. In summer woodpeckers drill in the trees for bugs, while in autumn squirrels collect nuts and a wide assortment of fungi provides food and shelter for a diverse range of insects and invertebrates. In winter you may glimpse a shy roe deer through the trees.

The Giant's Hedge in Kilminorth Woods.

Just offshore is Looe Island, also known as St George's Island. There is a medieval chapel on the island, once a popular place for pilgrimages; but so many people drowned trying to reach it that a new Benedictine chapel was built across from it on the mainland, sometime around the twelfth century. The Lamanna Chapel, just a short detour uphill at Hannafore, was built on the site of a sixth-century Celtic monastery and incorporated a monk's cell. It was originally part of Glastonbury Abbey, but by the fourteenth century it was a private chantry chapel.

Looe harbour.

Talland's two tiny and secluded shingle beaches were much loved in the past by smugglers. It is thought likely that at the start of the eighteenth century they were aided and abetted by Talland's eccentric vicar, the Reverend Richard Dodge, a renowned exorcist who was often to be seen leaping around the churchyard at night, cracking a whip around the headstones to drive away evil spirits (or was it just a cover?).

The creek at Kilminorth.

Fowey

St Saviour's Hill

Polruan

Lantic Bay

Pencarrow Head

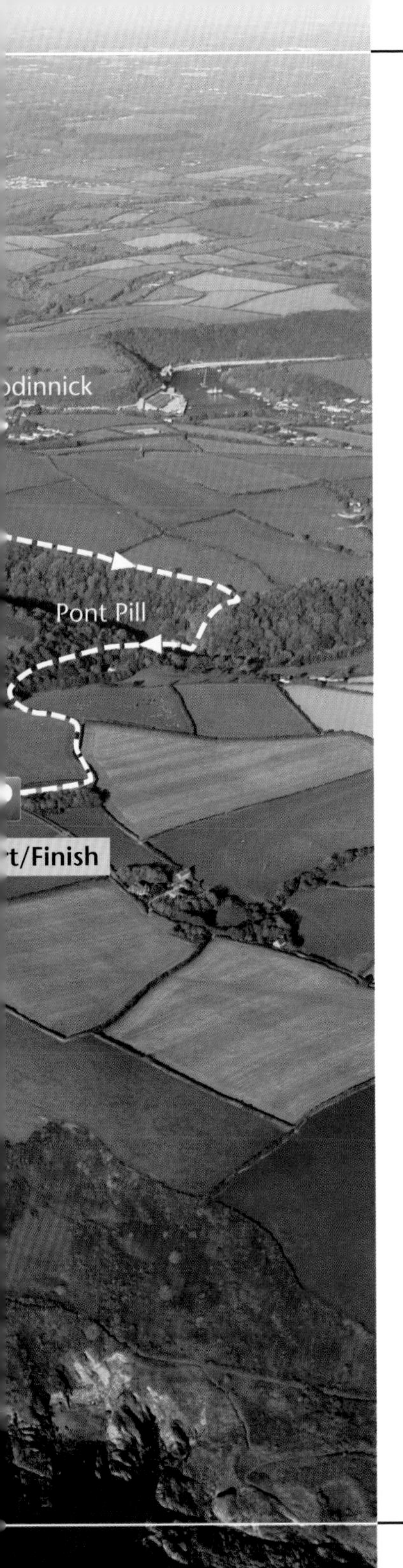

Walk 4 – Bodinnick, Polruan and Fowey

Distance	5.75 miles (8.5km)
Estimated time	2¾ hours
Difficulty	●●●●●
Ascent	1148ft (350m)
Map	OS Explorer Map 107
Starting point	SX 149513

Notes: A hard but delightful walk travelling high above Lantic Bay and crossing the River Fowey twice by ferry, giving wonderful views along both creeks as they wind between steep and ancient woodlands. There is an alternative route which avoids the ferry crossings. (For details of the alternative route as well as the ferries, see overleaf).

From the entrance to the Pencarrow car park turn left and walk to the junction to pick up the footpath on the opposite side of the road at the top. Follow the waymarkers to join the South West Coast Path above Lantic Bay. (Although it doesn't show as such on the OS map, the footpath is immediately opposite when you reach the top of the road.)

Turn right onto the Coast Path and follow it to Polruan, picking up the footpath on your left on St Saviour's Hill, to walk past the Coastwatch lookout before dropping downhill round the houses to come out on Battery Lane. Follow this around to the right, turning right on West Street and then left onto the quay to take the ferry across to Fowey.

Turn right on the Esplanade and right again on Lostwithiel Street, then right once more to keep alongside the river to the quay to take the ferry across to Bodinnick. Walk uphill past the Ferry

Pont Pill.

Inn to pick up the footpath on the right (Hall Walk). Follow Hall Walk through the woods and along the field boundary beyond, going over the stile to your right and dropping downhill to Pont Pill, forking right on the way down.

Crossing the footbridge, carry on along the path ahead and climb steeply uphill to the road. Turn left and take the footpath on the right (signed to the church) and follow it to come out on the road by Lanteglos Church. Turn left here and walk about half a mile to the car park.

Hall Chapel was built in the fourteenth century and was part of Hall Manor, which belonged to the Mohun family, Barons of Dunster in Somerset. The chapel was constructed of local slate with the mouldings around the doors and windows formed of Pentewan stone. A bell turret was added in the following century.

THE NATIONAL TRUST

HALL WALK IS WRITTEN OF BY CAREW IN HIS SURVEY OF CORNWALL, PUBLISHED IN 1602, AS A PLACE OF DIVERSIFIED PLEASINGS. IT WAS HERE THAT DURING THE CIVIL WAR ON THE 17TH AUGUST 1644, KING CHARLES NARROWLY ESCAPED DEATH WHEN A SHOT KILLED A POOR FISHERMAN WHO WAS STANDING AT A PLACE WHERE THE KING HAD STOOD BUT A SHORT WHILE BEFORE. IT IS HOPED THAT GENERATIONS TO COME WILL FIND ITS PROSPECTS PLEASING AS DID CAREW AND WILL RESPECT ITS USAGE ACCORDINGLY.

During the Reformation the chapel was decommissioned and converted for domestic use. By the nineteenth century it was being used as a farm building, and after the roof blew off in a storm in 1976 the whole building began to disintegrate.

Another ruined chapel encountered on this walk is the eighth-century St Saviour's Chapel, beside the Coastwatch lookout at Polruan. As well as being a useful lookout and informal lighthouse, it was an important place for pilgrims travelling to Santiago de Compostela in Spain. On the cliffs below is Punche's Cross, built as a warning to sailors. The cross appears on very early shipping charts and was repaired by monks from Tywardreath if it was damaged by storms.

The well-preserved blockhouse at Polruan is one of a pair on either side of the River Fowey. These were built at the end of the fourteenth century, when Edward III ordered that a chain should be stretched across the mouth of the port as a defence against French ships. In 1457 the French launched a raid on Fowey Harbour, regardless, and a boom defence was added as a result. There was a tower on each blockhouse, with separate staircases between ground floor and first floor, and first floor and battlements.

The Cornish writer Arthur Quiller-Couch, who wrote under the pseudonym 'Q', was born in Bodmin and lived in Fowey. Quiller-Couch was best known for his literary criticism and his Oxford Book of English Verse 1250-1900. Q's friend, Kenneth Graham, would visit him here, and it is said that Graham's Wind in the Willows was set in Lerryn, upriver from Fowey, and that Ratty was based on Q, who liked nothing better than to mess about in boats.

Author Daphne du Maurier was married in Lanteglos Church in 1932, and it featured as 'Lanoc Church' in her first novel, The Loving Spirit. The name Lanteglos comes from the Cornish 'nant eglos', meaning 'church valley'. From 1926 until 1943, du Maurier lived in Ferryside, to the right of the ferry slipway at Bodinnick. Her Cornish novels, Jamaica Inn, Rebecca and Frenchman's Creek were all written here (see pages 26 & 27).

Quiller Couch Monument at Hall Walk.

Ferries and the alternative route

The route described makes use of the two ferries which run regular crossings between Polruan and Fowey, and Fowey and Bodinnick. Details are on the South West Coast Path website at www.southwestcoastpath.com/ferries

For an alternative route which does not cross the river, continue around the quay at Polruan, walking up East Street to take the steps on the right signed 'Hall Walk' and follow the path through the trees and down to Pont. Cross the footbridge and carry on around Hall Walk, bearing left in the field to drop back into the woods, until you come to the path on the right a short way after the 'Q' monument. Follow the waymarkers past Hall Chapel and through fields to rejoin the Hall Walk at the stile to the woods above Pont Pill. From here follow the main route back to Lantic Bay.

Coombe
Start/Finish
P
Polridmouth
Lankelly Cliff
Southground Cliffs
Southground Point
Coomb Haven

Walk 5 – St Catherine's Castle

Distance	2.5 miles (4.25km)
Estimated time	1½ hours
Difficulty	●●○○○
Ascent	467ft (142m)
Map	OS Explorer Map 107
Starting point	SX 110511

Notes: Occupying a prime location with spectacular views over the river and its creeks as well as out to sea, St Catherine's Castle has been guarding Fowey since prehistoric times. A short walk on tracks and paths with brief stretches of fairly steep ascent and descent.

WALK 5

From the entrance of the National Trust car park at Coombe take the footpath along the lane to the right, following it through Allday's Fields and down along the edge of Readymoney Wood.

Reaching a T-junction on the track at the bottom, turn right, dropping downhill and then turning right again a short distance further on, to join the South West Coast Path as it curves around St Catherine's Castle above St Catherine's Point.

Drop down into Coombe Haven and then climb steeply on the far side above Southground Cliffs and then Lankelly Cliff, with the daymark tower on Gribbin Head in front of you. Turning inland and descending to the cove at Polridmouth, turn right onto the footpath before you reach the lake, and follow it back up to the car park, about a mile beyond.

Polkerris
Tregaminion
Trena
Menabilly
Little Gribbin
Gribbin Head

Walk 6 – Lankelly and Menabilly

Distance	5 miles (8km)
Estimated time	2½ hours
Difficulty	●●●●●●
Ascent	544ft (166m)
Map	OS Explorer Map 107
Starting point	SX 110511

Notes: A longish, but not too arduous stroll around Daphne du Maurier country, with some Arthurian legend, ancient crosses and prehistoric associations thrown in. The paths travel through fields and woodland as well as around the coast, with a short stretch on a quiet country lane.

From the National Trust car park at Coombe take the footpath leading from the bottom right-hand corner, heading south west, and follow it down to the cove at Polridmouth.

Turn right onto the South West Coast Path and follow it around Gribbin Head, past the daymark tower, and on for about 1½ miles to Polkerris.

As the Coast Path curves around behind Polkerris Beach, turn right onto the path heading inland to the road. Turn right and then left a short distance further, in front of Tregaminion Church. Follow the waymarkers for the Saints' Way, taking note of the direction signs through the farmyard to come out into the fields beyond.

The footpath crosses a stream and heads uphill, dropping to another stream and climbing a long flight of steps before passing through Trenant. Then it follows the edge of fields before a stone stile takes you onto a holloway leading downhill through the woods and under a bridge.

The beach at Coombe Haven.

From here it climbs to the houses. Turn right onto Combe Lane, at the top, and walk about ½ mile back to the car park.

At the side of the B3415, just outside Fowey, is the Tristan Stone. Erected around AD 550, on the north side it is inscribed with a T (an early form of the Christian cross), while on the south side the sixth-century lettering reads: 'DRASTANS HIC LACIT, CVNOWORI FILIVS'. The plaque beside the stone, added by the Fowey Old Cornwall Society, translates this as 'Trystan here lies, of Cunomorus the son'.

According to the plaque, Cunomorus was Mark of Cornwall in the Arthurian love story of Tristan and Iseult. The stone has been associated with Castle Dore, an Iron Age hillfort a few miles to the north, where a nearby henge is thought to be Bronze Age and the original site of the Tristan Stone. The hillfort was reoccupied in the fifth to eighth centuries AD, and traces of a wooden structure have been found which are said to have been King Mark's hall from that time.

Following Henry VIII's Reformation and his rift with Rome, England came under increasing threat from French and Spanish fleets, and Henry commissioned a new blockhouse at St Catherine's Point to replace the earlier pair of blockhouses on either side of the river (see pages 20 & 21). Built between 1538 and 1540 on a platform in the rock giving it commanding views over the water, the two-storey blockhouse capitalised on the protection provided by the precipitous cliffs on either side of the bastion and curtain wall.

Major refurbishments were carried out to the castle during the Crimean War in 1855, and during the Second World War St Catherine's Point was further modified. After the war the site was dismantled.

The 84-foot red-and-white striped daymark tower at Gribbin Head was built in 1832 to warn ships of the rocks below. It belongs to the National Trust and is occasionally open on a Sunday in the summer for the visitor with a head for heights and a willingness to ascend the steep and narrow staircase in order to enjoy the panoramic views at the top of the tower.

Daphne du Maurier

Menabilly was the inspiration for Manderley, the house at the centre of Daphne du Maurier's novel *Rebecca*. The author fell in love with the Fowey estuary in 1926, when her parents bought Ferryside at Bodinnick, and in 1943, with her husband away at war, she rented Readymoney House in Fowey for herself and her children. Two years later she and her husband, Major (later Lieutenant-General Sir) Frederick Browning, moved to Menabilly. After Browning died in 1965 she moved to another Fowey house owned by the family, Kilmarth. This became the setting for her novel *A House on the Strand.*

Daphne du Maurier wrote her first novel, *The Loving Spirit*, when she was in her early twenties. It was brought out by a major publishing house, and was an instant success. Her subsequent novels were also bestsellers, and Alfred Hitchcock's 1940 film of *Rebecca* made her world famous, as well as winning the Best Picture Oscar in 1941.

She wrote many other novels set in Cornwall, as well as a number of plays, biographies, and histories, including *Vanishing Cornwall.*

She adopted Castle Dor, started by Arthur Quiller-Couch but incomplete when he died, and turned it into a novel based on the Tristan and Iseult legend and centred on Castle Dore.

Gribbin Head.

Kilhallon
Par
Par Beach
Start/Finis

Walk 7 – Par Beach

Distance	4.75 miles (7.5km)
Estimated time	2¼ hours
Difficulty	●●●●●
Ascent	316ft (96m)
Map	OS Explorer Map 107
Starting point	SX 086532

Notes: A gentle stroll on paths and quiet lanes, through sand dunes and nature reserves, past a lake teeming with seabirds and waterfowl. Some paths may be wet, so good footwear is advisable.

Walk through the Par Beach and St Andrews Road nature reserves from east to west and pick up the South West Coast Path to the main A3082 road. On the road turn left to go under the railway bridge to the footpath on the right along the lane by the caravan park. Cross the railway and then the road on this path and carry on a short way, to the footpath on your right. Follow this lane to the road at Kilhallon, turning right and then bearing right, to the crossroads beyond.

Continue ahead on the road and then on the lane beyond as the road turns left. Ignore the track to the left to continue ahead and bear right on the path, past the buildings, to the road at Treesmill.

Turn right and follow the road, over the railway bridge and past two turnings on the left, into Tywardreath. Bear right on Castledore Road as it joins from the left, continuing ahead along Mount Bennett Road and then Fore Street. Turn left onto Well Street, carrying on over Tywardreath Hill and down to the main A3082 Polmear road. Turn left and pass under the bridge to turn right and return to the car park.

Porthpean
Castle Gotha
Ropehaven
Start/Finish
Trevissick
Trenarran
Hallane
Drennick

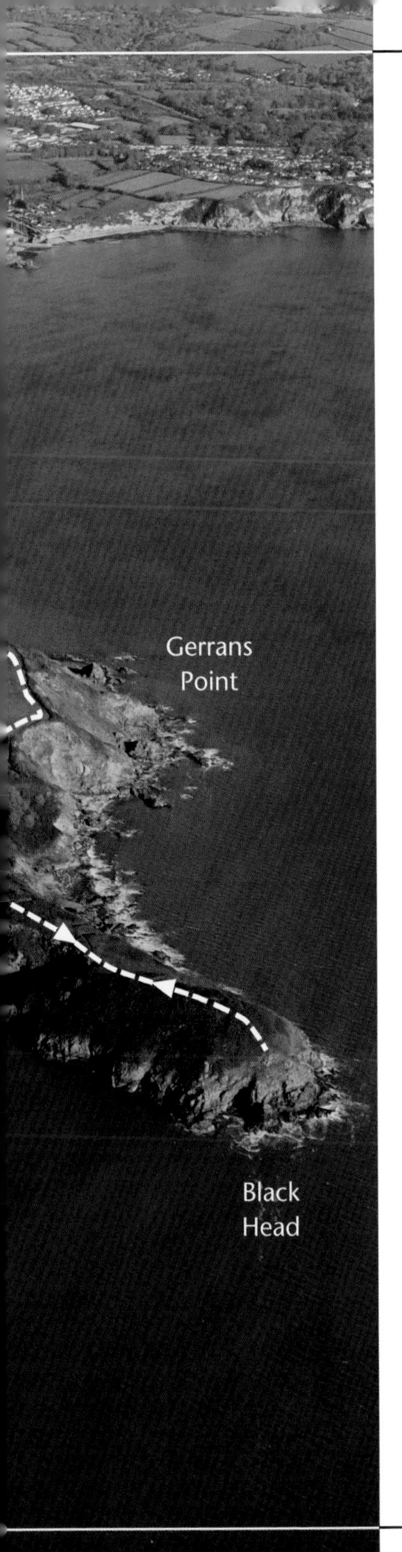

Walk 8 – Black Head and Castle Gotha

Distance	4.5 miles (7km)
Estimated time	2½ hours
Difficulty	●●●●●
Ascent	713ft (217m)
Map	OS Explorer Map 105
Starting point	SX 032489

Notes: A figure of eight around the remnants of two Iron Age forts, one a promontory fort and one a hillfort, with a loop through the Ropehaven Nature Reserve. A workout of a walk, with flat stretches interspersed with some steep ascent and descent, and in places the paths can be slippery after rain.

From the car park at Ropehaven walk south along the road, forking right to pass through Trenarran and following the lane down to the cottage above the beach at Hallane. Cross the bridleway and turn left over the stile just before the cottage, to follow the South West Coast Path uphill and over Drennick. The path runs high, past the A. L. Rowse commemorative stone. Detour here to visit Black Head.

Carry on along the Coast Path around Gerrans Point, ignoring the paths to the left, until you come back to the road and the car park. Head north on the road to the left-hand bend, and turn right onto the footpath through the field.

Follow the footpath along the hedge, and in the next field through the far hedge a little left of centre. To your right here as you enter the third field is the site of the ancient Castle Gotha, indicated by a semi-circle of hedges. Head for the gate in the left-hand hedge, leading to the road.

Looking across to Black Head.

Turning right, walk a few yards down the road to take the lane on your right leading to the modern-day Castle Gotha. Bear right with the lane, and take the footpath on the left just before the buildings and walk to the diagonally opposite corner, going through into the field beyond and dropping downhill to join the Coast Path at the bottom of the hill. Turn right on the Coast Path and follow it through the nature reserve, back to the car park.

According to the granite memorial stone on Black Head, Arthur Leslie Rowse was 'Lef a Gernow', the 'Voice of Cornwall', and he was made a Companion of Honour in 1996. His father was a china clay worker and uneducated, and Rowse was the first Cornishman to win a university scholarship.

Born in 1903, Rowse was a noted historian and poet, and his autobiography, A Cornish Childhood, brought him celebrity and a worldwide demand for his services as a speaker. Despite this, however, he remained adamantly Cornish and spent much of his life here, living and dying at Trenarran. 'This was the land of my content', reads his memorial stone.

Ropehaven Nature Reserve.

Castle Gotha was an Iron Age settlement, constructed during the second century BC and inhabited for some 400 years. Archaeologists found the sites of timber huts, just inside the rampart, which they believe to have been occupied by metalworkers. They found an ingot mould embedded in the floor of one of the huts, and elsewhere pits, hearths and a stone mould for casting brooches were found.

Silvermine Point Beach.

Little is known about the promontory fort at Black Head, and little remains of it. Assumed to be Iron Age, like Castle Gotha, there are three lines of defence across the neck of the headland, although there is scarcely any trace of the outer rampart and ditch. The central and inner banks are a little over 5 metres high, fronted by ditches around 2 metres deep, and it is likely that this was a defensive site, unlike Castle Gotha.

Purchased in 1986 with the help of a grant from the World Wildlife Fund, the Ropehaven Nature Reserve is particularly noted for its birds and its geology. The cliffs are among the oldest sedimentary rocks exposed in the southwest, having been laid down some 400 million years ago, and as well as being steep they are prone to landslides. Combined with the coastal woodland, this makes for a range of habitats between the Coast Path and the shoreline.

The rocks are rich in fossils, indicating that Ropehaven once lay under tropical seas, where coral reefs were home to sea lilies, shellfish and primitive squid and fish. Other geological features include old slate workings and thin bands of limestone, a rock which is not widely found in Cornwall.

The Saints' Way

The Saints' Way ('Forth an Syns' in Cornish) is a 28-mile walking route that runs along the River Camel, linking ancient trade routes between Fowey and Padstow on Cornwall's north coast. The complete trail was devised between 1984 and 1986 after two local walkers stumbled upon a series of granite stiles and began to investigate the old paths and holloways crisscrossing the county. Some of the ancient paths that make up the trail link crosses, shrines, holy wells, chapels and churches with Neolithic hill forts and Bronze Age standing stones, and would have been used by the early Celtic saints and missionaries.

The long-distance trail is also known as the Drovers' Way and the Mariners' Way, as many of its constituent paths were used by drovers, traders and pilgrims. Others would have been adopted by merchants bringing gold from Ireland to the Mediterranean via Cornwall and Brittany, and it has been suggested that even before the Iron Age the locals were trading with visitors from Egypt, Greece and Phoenicia.

Peruppa
Farm
Heligan
Mill
Cheesewarne
Farm
Start/Finish
P
Mevagissey

Walk 9 – Mevagissey and Heligan Mill

Distance	5 miles (8.25km)
Estimated time	2½ hours
Difficulty	•••••
Ascent	749ft (228m)
Map	OS Explorer Map 105
Starting point	SX 012450

Notes: Fairly long and with some ascent and descent, this walk includes the medieval settlement associated with the famous Lost Gardens of Heligan. Pause for lunch in Pentewan, just off-route, once one of Cornwall's busiest china clay ports with the remains still visible around the harbour.

From the car park entrance in Mevagissey turn right and walk up Valley Road (B3273) to where Church Lane joins from the right. Just after the junction take the footpath along the lane on the left, past the sports centre and running almost parallel to the road. Ignore turnings to left and then right as the lane sweeps around Cheesewarne Farm, and fork left to follow the footpath through the trees to Heligan Mill.

Do not cross the footbridge but bear right to walk northwards, turning left and then bearing left to follow the path uphill to a T-junction. Turn left on the road, bearing left again a moment later to follow the path along the hedge, continuing ahead on the lane beyond to the road.

Turn left and walk to Peruppa Farm, picking up the footpath on the right opposite the buildings. Hugging the wood through the first two fields, turn right immediately you enter the third field, to follow the footpath east towards the road,

Mevagissey harbour.

turning right in the last field and then left onto the lane to the B3273.

Turn right and walk about ¾ mile along the road, past the holiday park, to pick up the South West Coast Path on your left above the end of the beach, and follow it to Mevagissey. Drop down to the harbour and walk along The Cliff and into Mevagissey to make your way back to the car park.

A picturesque fishing village, Mevagissey was first recorded as a hamlet in 1313, although there is evidence of settlement dating back to the Bronze Age. In the fourteenth century it was known as Porthilly, but towards the end of the fifteenth century it merged with the neighbouring hamlet at Lamoreck, and the new village was named after two Irish saints, St Meva and St Issey ('Meva hag Issey' in Cornish, 'hag' meaning 'and').

Like many Cornish fishing villages, in the seventeenth century the port's main sources of income were pilchards and smuggling. Many of the buildings around the seafront were associated with the sea and shipping, such as a boatyard, a cooper's workshop, a fish merchant's shop and assorted warehouses.

It is said to have been the first town in England to have electric street lamps. In 1895 The Mevagissey Electric Supply Company built a power station on West Quay to burn the oil pressed from the pilchards when they were processed, powering the lighthouse too.

Pentewan slipway.

Mevagissey Bay.

Past Mevagissey celebrities included Andrew Pears, founder of Pears Soap, who was born here in 1768 and set up a barber's shop before moving to London. Twentieth-century author Susan Cooper used the village as the setting for two of the novels in her The Dark is Rising series, after childhood holidays spent here. She renamed it Trewissick, and the former rectory Mevagissey House was the model for the vicarage in Over Sea Under Stone.

Described by sixteenth-century antiquary John Leland as 'a sandy bay witherto fischer bootes repair for socour', Pentewan was once a bustling harbour which shipped a third of Cornwall's china clay, as well as sand and stone, and brought in limestone and cement, and coal for the tin and clay mines. Another import was Baltic timber for barrel-making.

Pentewan's first harbour, built in 1744, had fallen into disrepair by the end of the century, but in 1826 a new harbour was built for the china clay industry, with a deep-cut basin and a tidal channel, with lock gates and a breakwater added in 1831. However, the district's mining activities caused the river to silt up, and in the 1920s a sand and block works was established beside it to use some of this material; but the process continued, and the last trading ship left the harbour in 1940. By the 1960s even small pleasure boats were unable to get through. The harbour is now completely cut off from the sea and contains only freshwater.

Tracks and sidings from the railway still run inland from the beach, and the lock gates and breakwater are now Grade II listed features.

The settlement at Heligan Mill was first recorded in 1356, when it was spelt 'Helyganmille', and it is thought that there was a mill here from that time. Heligan (meaning 'willows' in Cornish) was the seat of the Tremayne family for more than 400 years and is famous for its 'Lost Gardens'. These were gardens created by the family from the middle of the eighteenth century which were abandoned after most of the gardeners were lost in the First World War. Neglected for over 75 years, the gardens were restored in the 1990s.

A Romano-British brooch and ring were found in the Polmassick river near Heligan in 1787, thought to be from the sixth century and imported from Ireland, suggesting that Heligan was inhabited as long ago as the Iron Age.

Portmellon

Trewollock

Gorran Haven

P Start/Finish

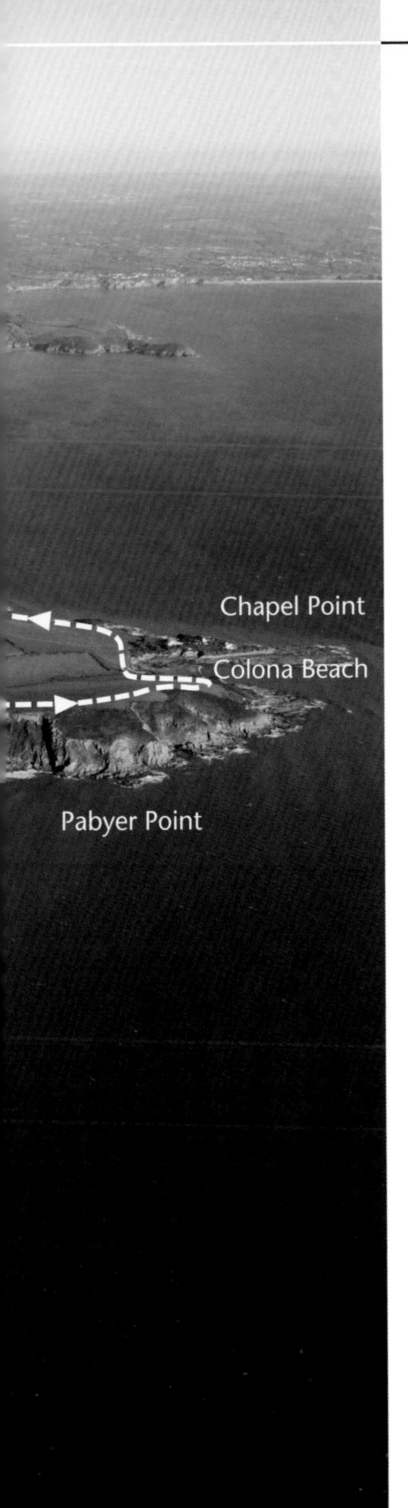

Walk 10 – Portmellon

Distance	3.75 miles (6km)
Estimated time	1¾ hours
Difficulty	●●●●●
Ascent	477ft (145m)
Map	OS Explorer Map 105
Starting point	SX 010415

Notes: A walk through traditional fishing and boat-building territory, with some far-reaching coastal views and an inland community woodland. Most of the walk is on paths and lanes, with a short stretch along a quiet road.

From the car park at Gorran Haven walk down towards the beach. Turn left onto Church Street and then take the second right, to walk along Cliff Road. Turn left onto the South West Coast Path and follow it out to Pabyer Point and then around Colona Beach and Chapel Point to the cove at Portmellon.

The Coast Path drops onto the road past the first houses and comes to a T-junction. Turn right and follow the road around to the left. Take the first turning on the left, bearing right to pick up the footpath on your right, heading along the valley and curving left into the trees.

Coming to the lane by the houses turn left and walk eastwards to the road. Turn right and then left onto the footpath about 100 yards beyond, dropping gently down through the first field to climb back up to the road in the second. Turn left on the road, forking left to continue in the same direction a little further on.

At Trewollock take the footpath on the left, bearing right immediately to drop downhill

Gorran Haven beach.

along the lane and then through the field beyond, to return on Cliff Road. Retrace your steps to the car park.

The early Cornish name for Gorran Haven was 'Porth Ust', or 'St Just's Cove', and the fifteenth-century church is dedicated to St Just. With a 110-foot tower designed as a landmark for sailors, it is thought to have been built by Sir Henry Bodrugan in around 1475.

The chapel was seized by the Crown under Henry VIII's 1547 Chantries Act, when commissioners were sent to confiscate land as well as gold and silver from all chantries (or private chapels), and it was sold in 1568. Its subsequent secular roles included use as a fisherman's store, and by the middle of the eighteenth century, when the Reverend Richard Dalby was appointed Vicar of Gorran, it had fallen into disrepair. Dalby had it restored around 1780 and during the nineteenth century it was used by Congregationalists for their services. In 1862, it passed into the hands of the Anglican vicars of St Gorran, whose fifteenth-century parish church is about a mile inland in the little village of Gorran.

Turbot Point, on the headland between Gorran Haven and Portmellon, is also known as Bodrugan's Leap. Bodrugan Barton, no more than a mile from the point, was listed in the Domesday Book of 1086 as having 'land for 10 ploughs, woodland 4 acres, pasture 200 acres' and was sufficiently significant in the Middle Ages to be called Bodrugan Castle.

Chapel Point.

Sir Henry Bodrugan was a notoriously brutal henchman of Richard III in his battle against Henry Tudor for the English throne in the fifteenth century. Bodrugan (also known as Trenowth) was sent by his overlord to Cotehele, to dispatch Tudor supporter Sir Richard Edgcumbe. According to local legend, the latter made his escape by throwing his hat into the river and hiding behind a tree, whereupon the king's men departed, assuming that he had drowned.

When Henry succeeded in seizing the throne, becoming Henry VII, Bodrugan was charged with treason and the roles were reversed. Bodrugan fled to Turbot Point, with Edgcumbe in hot pursuit, and he is said to have leapt from the cliff-top to a boat waiting in the bay below to convey him to France. Most of Bodrugan's estates, including St Gorran, were confiscated and handed over to Edgcumbe.

St Just Chapel of Ease.

Boat-building in Portmellon

The whole area has a long history of boatbuilding and was particularly noted for making warships for the Napoleonic Wars, as well as smaller vessels fast enough to outrun the revenue men. Portmellon's boatyards made an important contribution to this reputation, and many famous wooden-hulled boats left the port.

Boat-builder Percy Mitchell, born in 1901, ran a yard here after he took over his employer's business in Mevagissey in the 1920s and moved it to Portmellon, where it was easier to launch the boats. He was described as 'one of the finest traditional boat-builders in the world', and 'an artist in wood', before the economics of wooden boatbuilding saw the yard close in 1983.

His first commission, the *Ibis*, was one of the biggest fishing luggers to work from Mevagissey, and its catch numbers made the record books, including the largest ever haul of pilchards, at a monstrous 2346 stones (almost 15,000 kilograms). During the Second World War he built motor cutters and boats for the Admiralty, acquiring a reputation that made his boats much sought-after. One of his most famous ships was the 28-ton Windstar, which often carried King George V and the young Princess Elizabeth.

Gorran Ha

Hemmick Beach

Penare

Dodman Point

Walk 11 – Dodman Point

Distance	4.75 miles (7.75km)
Estimated time	2½ hours
Difficulty	●●●●●
Ascent	863ft (263m)
Map	OS Explorer Map 105
Starting point	SX 010415

Notes: A strenuous but superb walk from the small fishing village of Gorran Haven, with its tiny sheltered beach and the fishing boats, past the great open stretch of Bow Beach and around Dodman Point, the highest point on Cornwall's southern coastline. There are some stretches of steep ascent and descent with a long flight of steps.

From the car park at Gorran Haven drop downhill towards the beach, turning right to take the South West Coast Path up the steps on Foxhole Lane, heading towards Hemmick via Dodman. Follow the path through the National Trust land at Lamledra, bearing left when a path leads uphill, and carry on above Vault Beach to the bulwark across Dodman Point.

Going through the gate, carry on along the Coast Path around Dodman Point. At the stone cross, there is a shortcut on the path heading inland, which runs along the top of the ridge, past the old lookout cottage, and goes through another gate on the bulwark to follow a track to the road at Penare.

For the longer route, carry on along the Coast Path, initially dropping steeply downhill and then descending more gently to the road above Hemmick Beach.

Bow or Vault Beach.

Turn right onto the footpath that runs above the road, climbing steeply uphill to Penare, and drop onto the road by Penare Farm. Carry on along the road, turning left when the track joins from Dodman Point (or bearing right if you have taken the shortcut and arrived on this track).

Coming to the T-junction, carry straight ahead along the footpath through the campsite to the road to Treveague Farm. Turn right here to pick up the footpath on the left by the buildings and walk down to Gorran Haven. Turn right on Rice Lane and then bear left to return to the car park.

The picturesque thirteenth-century whitewashed and bare-stone cottages of Gorran Haven huddle around steep and narrow streets in the lee of the 370-foot high Dodman Point. The Point has been an important site throughout history, and the

Signal House on Dodman Point.

archaeological remains found here include Bronze Age barrows, Iron Age fortifications, medieval field systems and a Napoleonic signal station, as well as the enormous Victorian cross. This was erected in 1896 as a navigation aid for shipping and visible for many miles out to sea. Originally made of granite, the cross was struck by lightning but repaired by the Earl of Edgcumbe.

Signal House, in among the gorse bushes just a few metres behind the cross, was built in 1794 on an Armada beacon site, and was part of a chain of coastal signal stations built to keep a lookout for French ships in the Channel.

Some 2,000 years ago, the local people built an enormous double rampart from cliff to cliff across the tip of the peninsula, over 2 metres high on the outside bank and as much as 2 metres in places on the inside. Overall the bulwark was some 900 metres in length and enclosed nearly 50 acres of land, making it the longest ditch and rampart of any promontory fort in Cornwall.

The logistics involved in building such a large fortification show how vulnerable this coastline was felt to be against attack by raiders, and the promontory was called into service as a lookout and an early-warning base in later centuries too.

Cornish Stone Crosses

There are over 400 stone crosses in Cornwall, and the fragmentary remains of at least 200 more. The most common are wayside crosses, standing at the side of roads, trackways and paths. In medieval times these marked the route to the parish church, or to a pilgrimage or monastic site, an ancient chapel or a holy well. The most elaborate crosses are found in Cornwall's churchyards. In many cases the burial ground existed before the church, and the cross was used to mark the site.

Sometimes stone crosses were placed beside rivers, to mark a safe place for crossing. On the coast, as at Dodman Point, this function of keeping wayfarers safe was met through the use of crosses to mark rocks or cliffs by day, while chapels or monks' cells on the cliffs kept a light burning to warn sailors by night.

In the Dark Ages, local kings or chieftains sometimes had inscribed memorial crosses raised to them, such as the famous ninth-century King Doniert Stone at St Cleer, or the Tristan Stone outside Fowey (see pages 26–27).

Celtic cross in a Cornish graveyard.

A more mundane function of stone crosses was to mark the boundaries of a parish, or of glebe land. In post-medieval times they were also sometimes used to show manorial or domestic boundaries, with personal initials carved.

Large crosses were also set up in villages, often in the market place, and became the focal point.

Many take the form of the Celtic cross, also known as the wheeled cross. It has been suggested that St Patrick (or possibly St Declan) devised this by combining the Christian cross with the pagan sun cross, using the hybrid to impress upon pagan converts the important life-giving properties of Christianity.

PORTHLUNNEY

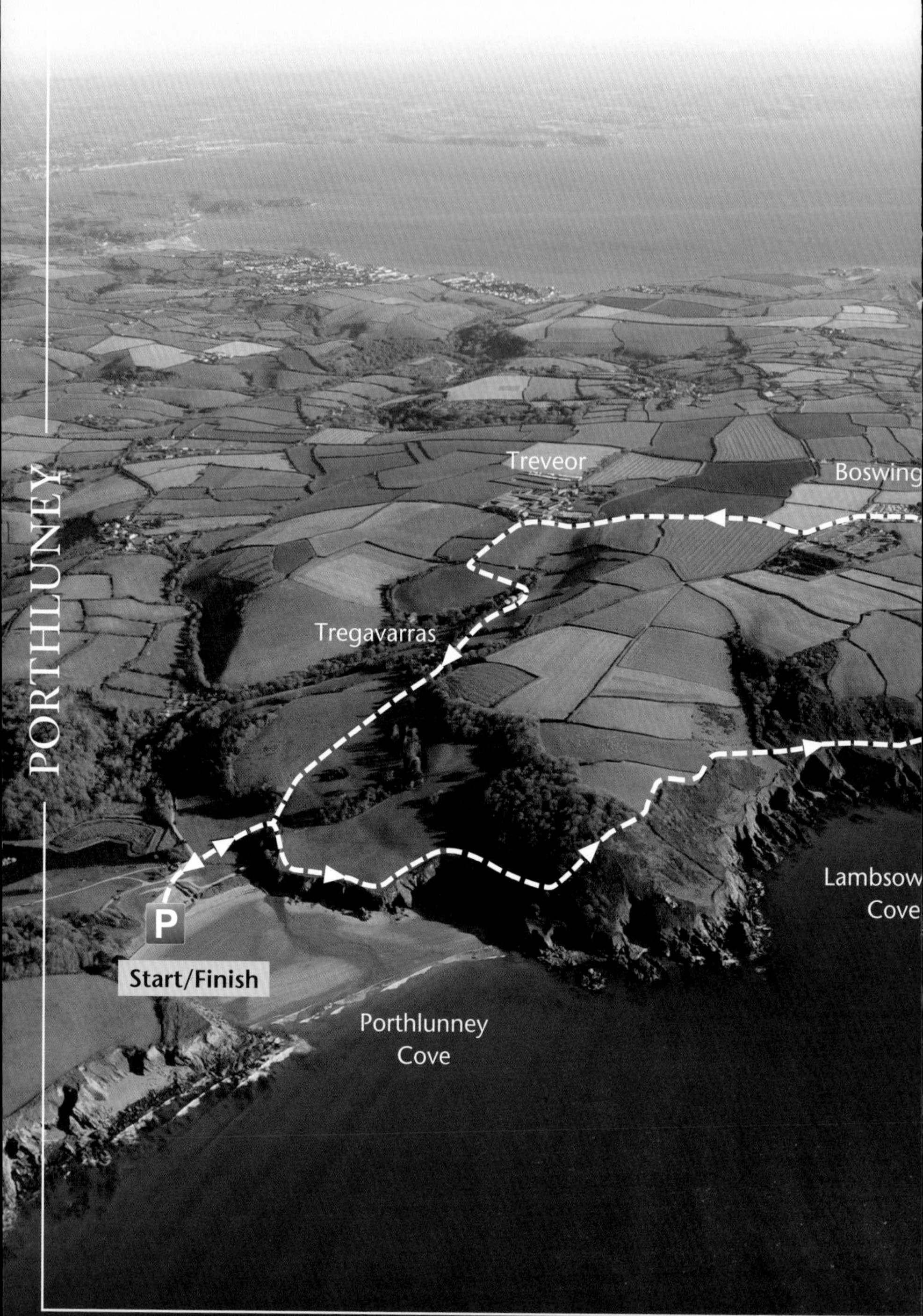

Walk 12 – Porthluney

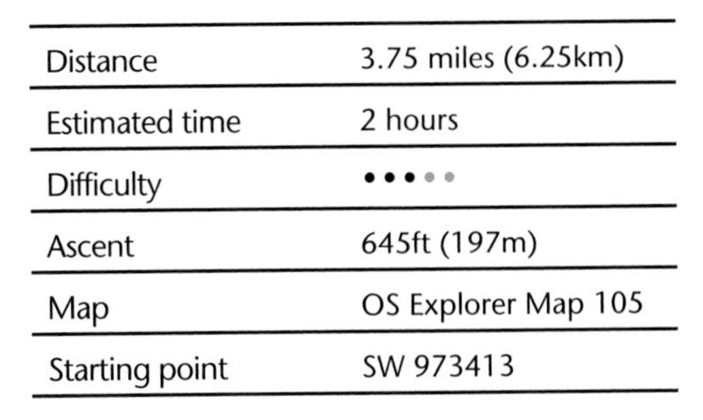

Distance	3.75 miles (6.25km)
Estimated time	2 hours
Difficulty	●●●●●
Ascent	645ft (197m)
Map	OS Explorer Map 105
Starting point	SW 973413

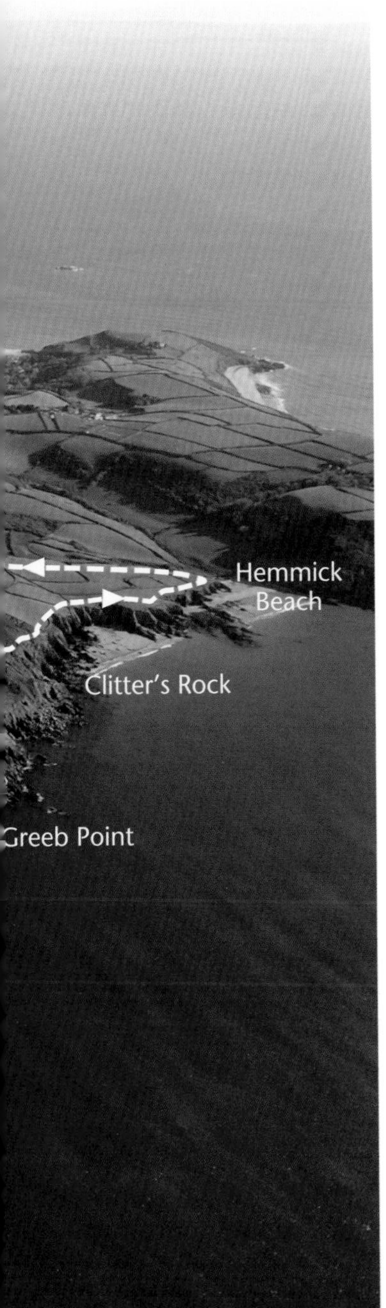

Notes: A fairly short walk featuring golden sands and a lavish country mansion designed by John Nash with a deer park and gardens that are internationally famous. There are stretches of ascent and descent, but only one is steep.

From the car park above Porthluney Cove return to the road and turn right, to pick up the South West Coast Path. This climbs a short distance and then turns to the right above the rocks at Porthluney before steeply ascending the small headland beyond. It sweeps around the coast above Lambsowden Cove and then Greeb Point, before curving around Clitter's Rock to drop gently to the road at Hemmick Beach.

Turn left and as the road curves to the left take the footpath on the right, heading uphill through two fields before bringing you back to the road again. Turn right and walk through Boswinger, bearing right to pass the youth hostel and then Boswinger Farm and carrying on past the turnings in the holiday park, to come out at a T-junction after the church. Turn left and take the footpath on the right a short distance further on, staying by the hedge to pick up a track heading gently downhill to Treveor.

Turn left on the road and walk about 250 yards to the right-hand bend. Turn left here onto the footpath and drop down to the trees near the left-hand corner, going through into the field beyond and turning right to walk past the row of houses. On the road bear left and carry on past the buildings at Tregavarras, picking up the footpath (not the lane) through the trees on your right when the road turns sharply left. Drop diagonally through this field to the road back to the car park at Porthluney.

Portloe.

The medieval manor of Caerhays, which can be seen from the start and end of the walk, belonged to the Arundells until around 1379, when it passed into the Trevanion family. When the last male Trevanion died in 1767, the Bettesworth family became the new owners, although John Bettesworth added the name Trevanion to his own.

In 1807 he had a new mansion built on the site of the manor house, designed by John Nash, the man responsible for Buckingham Palace and the Brighton Pavilion, and it was complemented by formal gardens with ornamental towers and follies.

In 1840 the cost of all this splendour presumably became too much for the Bettesworth-Trevanions, and they fled to Bruges, leaving Caerhays to the bailiffs. By the time Michael Williams bought the property in 1854, much of the castle was derelict and the gardens had run wild. He, and subsequently his son, set about restoration work, demolishing a number of buildings, filling in the mill leat, draining the Luney Valley moors, planting new woodland, purchasing new land and creating a deer park.

In 1880 John Charles Williams inherited Caerhays and set about extending the gardens and filling them with large

The rocks at Portloe.

quantities of plants, indulging a passion for daffodil breeding as well as the fashionable habit of importing exotic shrubs. Today his lavish collections of rhododendrons and camellias, as well as the National Magnolia Collection here, have given the gardens at Caerhays an international reputation as Britain's most exotic woodland.

Speckled Wood butterfly on the Coast Path.

Porthluney (Cornish 'porth leveny') means 'cove of the smooth river', and the River Luney is said to have once been navigable all the way to Polmassick. The beach is a designated Eurobeach, with its golden sand and safe swimming, and it was used in 1979 for the filming of Daphne du Maurier's Rebecca (see pages 26 & 27). Unlike many other local beaches, it is not used as a fishing port, or for other shipping, although small boats would once have carried local produce to the bigger ports at Mevagissey, Falmouth and Truro.

As suggested by the nearby Watchhouse Point, there is a watch house above Porthluney, built in the nineteenth century as a lookout station. Georgian in design, it is one of three stations built on this part of the coastline, the others being at Nare Point and Dodman Point.

Wildflowers on the East Cornish Coast

Wildflowers thrive on this part of the Cornish coast, thanks to the conservation strategies used by the National Trust and other bodies responsible for managing the coastal properties.

Bluebells, violets and primroses appear first among the ferns and bracken, followed later by a riot of colour as red campions, ragged robins, stitchworts, dandelions and buttercups are joined by coastal species – sea campion, thrift and scabious, Michaelmas and ox-eye daisies, the blue and purple pokers of the viper's bugloss.

Here and there it is possible to spot more unusual flowers: sea kale, with its fleshy leaves and its brilliant yellow petals; the small yellow pearls on the upright, spiky-leaved wild asparagus, which later turn to vivid red berries; even, if you are lucky, the pink-petalled centaury with its yellow stamens. This was not seen in Cornwall from 1962 until 2010, when it was discovered growing at Land's End.

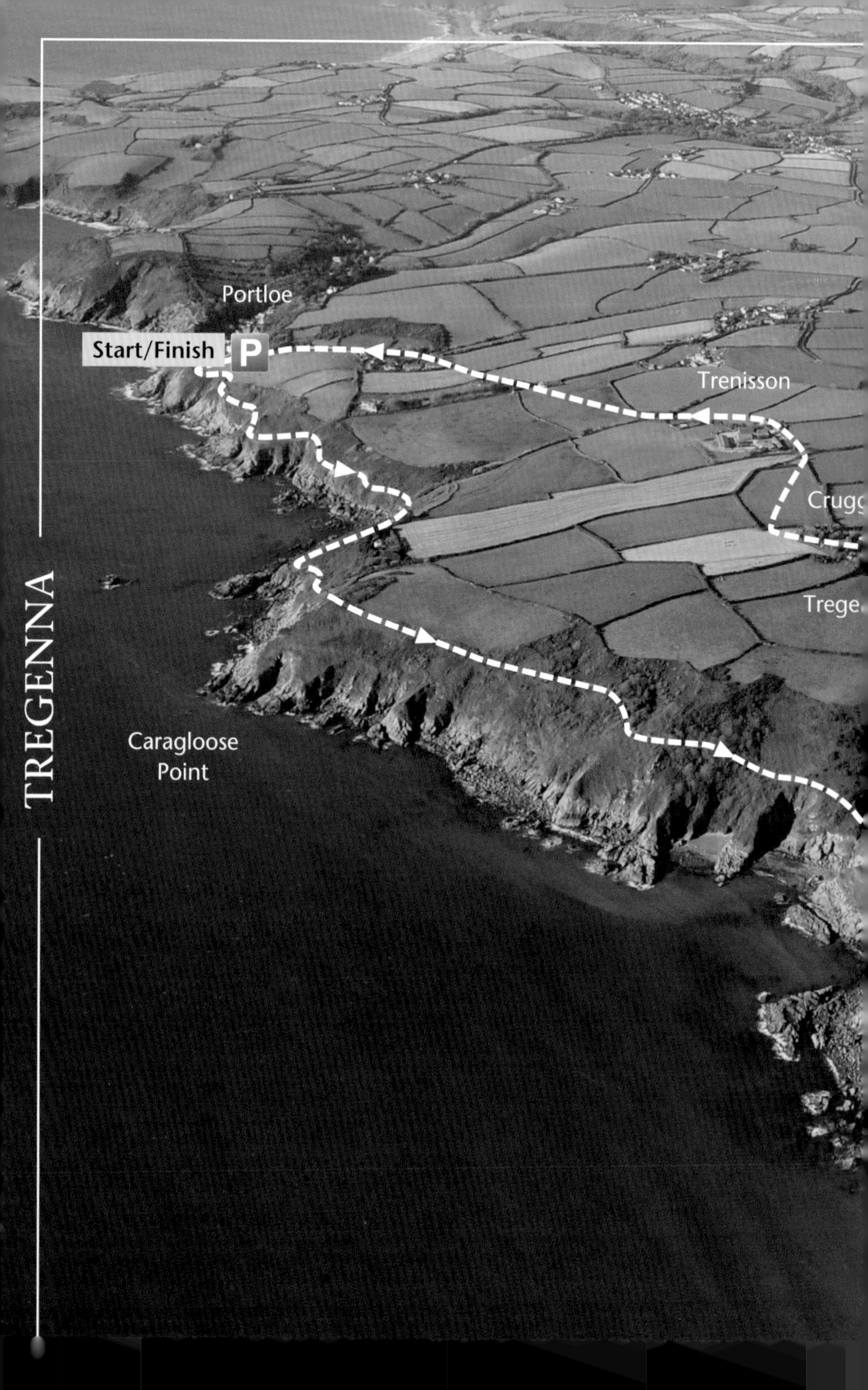
TREGENNA
Portloe
Start/Finish
P
Trenisson
Caragloose
Point

Walk 13 – Tregenna

Distance	3.25 miles (4.25km)
Estimated time	1½ hours
Difficulty	●●●●●
Ascent	525ft (160m)
Map	OS Explorer Map 105
Starting point	SW 938394

Notes: A short walk around a rocky coastline, with a lot of up and down but only one steep section. Portloe huddles in the small cove in the lee of steep hills and has been much-used as the backdrop for films and television dramas.

From the Carrick car park at Portloe walk towards the beach and pick up the South West Coast Path on the left and follow it past the old coastguard lookout to walk around a series of points and headlands for about a mile and a half, crossing a small stream before pulling out to the right at Caragloose Point.

Passing through National Trust land at Tregenna, cross a footbridge before turning inland to climb steeply to a T-junction. Leave the Coast Path here and head left on the lane, past a number of buildings, bearing left when it forks and turning left beyond, to follow the road to Tregenna Farm.

Between the buildings fork right and then left, turning right off the track in the field beyond to take the footpath through the next field to the farm track at Cruggan. Carry straight on ahead, following the track between the farm buildings and past Trenisson, to continue on the footpath through the field to the road beyond. Carry on ahead, downhill into Portloe and back to the car park.

Nare Head
Tregagle's
Hole
Carne
Start/Finish
Kiberick
Cove

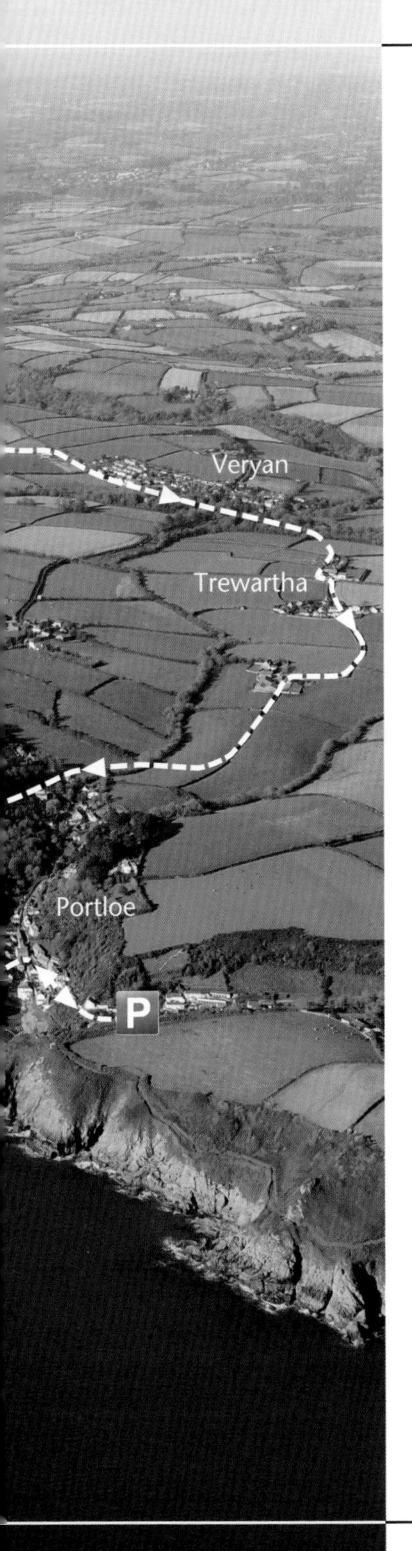

Walk 14 – Nare Head

Distance	5.75 miles (9.25km)
Estimated time	3 hours
Difficulty	●●●●●
Ascent	996 ft (304m)
Map	OS Explorer Map 105
Starting point	SW 921379

Notes: A fairly arduous hike with some stretches of steep ascent and descent, nonetheless this walk is not to be missed, with its wide-reaching views, across the water to Porthscatho and Falmouth in one direction and over land to St Austell's china clay hills.

From the National Trust car park at Kiberick Cove go through the gate to take the footpath steeply downhill towards the cove. Reaching the South West Coast Path, turn right and follow it around Nare Head. Note the Cold War bunker site on your right about halfway between the car park and the point.

The path drops steeply downhill on the far side of Nare Head, passing a ruined building and crossing a small stream before climbing steeply past Tregagle's Hole. Fork right to leave the Coast Path as it drops downhill, and continue uphill to Carne. Fork right just before the first houses, bearing right beyond them to bear left at the main settlement, ignoring the turning on your right shortly afterwards.

Take the footpath straight ahead at the sharp left-hand bend, passing to the left of the tumulus at Carne Beacon, and head back to the road to pick up the footpath into the next field leading to the road beyond. The earthworks of Veryan Castle are towards the bottom of the hill to your left as you go through this field.

Towards Tregagle's Hole.

Turn right on the road and walk through Veryan, carrying straight on at the crossroads to turn right on the footpath which passes to the left of the church. The footpath climbs through fields and a few trees to come out on a lane leading to the road. Turn left and then almost immediately take the road on the right, continuing straight ahead at Trewartha to follow the lane to Trewartha Hall. Stay on the footpath as it passes between the buildings, heading for the far right-hand corner of the second field to cross the stream at Sunny Corner.

Coming out by the houses, bear right and then left, to take the footpath on the right which drops downhill to a track. Turn left on the track and then right to join the Coast Path, following it around the coast to Kiberick, retracing your footsteps uphill here to return to the car park.

The Veryan Cold War bunker was built in 1963 to monitor radioactivity in the event of air attacks. It was designed as a basic survival unit for three people for three weeks, giving them virtually total protection from radioactive fallout during that time.

After the collapse of the Soviet Union in 1991 brought the Cold War to an end, the bunker was abandoned. It was subsequently restored in a joint project between the National Trust and the Truro branch of the Royal Observer Corps and is open to visitors several times a year.

Jan Tregagle was a seventeenth-century Justice of the Peace who made many unpopular judgements and carried out numerous wicked deeds, as well as spying for the Parliamentary forces during the Civil War in a devoutly Royalist county. After his death a defendant unwisely summoned his spirit to court to give testimony, and Tregagle swore that he would not return to the dead.

From that day forth he was heard to howl when storms blew in from the Atlantic, and his spirit hunted on Bodmin Moor, sometimes as a black dog and at other times as a giant bird. Exorcists sent him to the bottomless Dozmary Pool on the moor to empty out all the water with a limpet shell. Astonishingly he succeeded and fled to the hermitage at Roche Rock. From here he was despatched to St Minver, where he was to weave ropes of sand; but residents complained about his howling, so he was banished again, this time to Helston, to carry sacks of sand from Bareppa to Porthleven. Here the devil tripped him up, he spilt the sand, and the area became landbound.

Fleeing once more from Helston, he ended up in a sea cave – Tregagle's Hole, – where to this day he can be heard crashing and howling in the sea cave deep beneath the land.

Veryan Castle, or the 'Ringarounds', is an Iron Age or Roman-British coastal fort just to the west of Carne Beacon. Unusually, it is not on a promontory, but a few hundred yards inland, on the eastern slope of the deep valley which emerges on Carne Beach. Little survives of the double ramparts and their dividing ditch.

The Cold War bunker hatch at Veryan.

Farmland at Nare Head.

Rock formation at Nare Head.

GERRANS BAY

Gerrans

Start/Finish P

Rosteague

Towan Beach

Walk 15 – Gerrans Bay

Distance	3.75 miles (6km)
Estimated time	1¾ hours
Difficulty	●●●●●
Ascent	272ft (83m)
Map	OS Explorer Map 105
Starting point	SW 873350

Notes: An easy stroll around a short coastal loop just south of Porthscatho and Gerrans, passing through the fourteenth-century manor of Rosteague, whose colourful history embraces a range of owners from one of Sir Walter Raleigh's captains to 'Mad Mary' Hartley.

From the entrance to the car park at Gerrans turn left, turning left again a little further on, through the field just before the holiday park. In the next field follow the right-hand boundary to the far right-hand corner and straight on ahead to join the South West Coast Path beyond.

Turn right and walk above the sea for about 1½ miles to Towan Beach. Turn right on the footpath up to the road at Porth. Turn right here, onto the signed bridleway, and follow it through Rosteague and back to Gerrans.

Porthscatho is another picturesque unspoilt fishing village. The whitewashed cottages cluster around the tiny harbour. The Porthscatho pilchards are no more, but the boats still go out fishing for mackerel and lobsters.

On the hillside above, the large octagonal medieval spire of the church at Gerrans is a striking landmark for sailors to use in their navigation.

Porthscatho harbour.

In early medieval times Gerrans was known as 'Eglosgeren' – 'St Geran's Church' – suggesting that there may have been a church here even before the one documented in 1201. The present-day church was rebuilt on Norman foundations in 1849, although the medieval tower and font were kept, and the original stones and windows were reused as far as possible. There is also a medieval cross in the churchyard.

St Geran, or St Gerent or St Gereint, was said to be the grandson of the legendary King Mark of Cornwall. Gereint was converted to Christianity by St Teilo, one of the many Irish saints who travelled through Cornwall on his way to Brittany during the Dark Ages. According to legend, 'King Geran of Dumnonia' was killed during the Battle of Catterick in 598 and was buried at Dingerein Castle (meaning 'Gereint's fort' in Cornish).

Pednvaden Lookout, near Porthscatho.

The castle lies a few miles north of Gerrans and is a bivallate (two-ditched) hillfort thought to date from somewhere between 800 BC and AD 400.

According to the traveller and antiquarian John Leland, writing around 1540, there was a fogou, or vault, 'within but a shot of the north side' of the castle, although there is no trace of it now. 'Fogou' is the Cornish word for 'cave', and there are a few such vaults in the county. Their purpose is unknown, but it has been suggested that they were refuges, storage chambers or ritual shrines.

Leland also noted that at Polingey there was a 'mille grinding with the tide'. Although there are no records of its age, it is thought that it was here by 1416, or possibly earlier, and the 1880 Ordnance Survey map shows a 'sea mill' across the creek, recording it as a corn mill and also showing a mill pond. The dam of the mill pond once carried a road from Tregassick to Lanhay, and there is still a footpath where it ran. At low tide it is still possible to see a causeway across the creek.

There are several tidal mills on the local creeks. A dam was built across a creek, which allowed the water to come in with the tide, but then held it behind sluice gates, allowing it through in a steady stream to power the mill. It was possible to use the sea's energy in this way for just five hours on each tide, so millers were required to work unsociable hours to make the most of the power.

There was also a tidal mill owned by the monks at Place, still working in 1812 but destroyed in 1860 and the pond filled in to make way for the lawn at Place House. Other similar mills existed at Froe and at the head of the Polingey creek.

At Porthcurnick, just north of Gerrans, there are the remains of a submerged forest, drowned when melting ice caused sea levels to rise after the last Ice Age and fossilised. It is sometimes possible to see the gnarled roots and a few large stumps at low tide, and fragments of Iron Age pottery have been found in its clay surface, dated at around the second century BC, as well as acorns and hazel nuts.

Froe Creek.

Porthcurnick Beach.

ST ANTHONY HEAD

St Mawes

North Hill Point

Start/Finish

Amsterdam Point

Cellars Beach

St Mawes Harbour

Carricknath Point

St Anthony Head

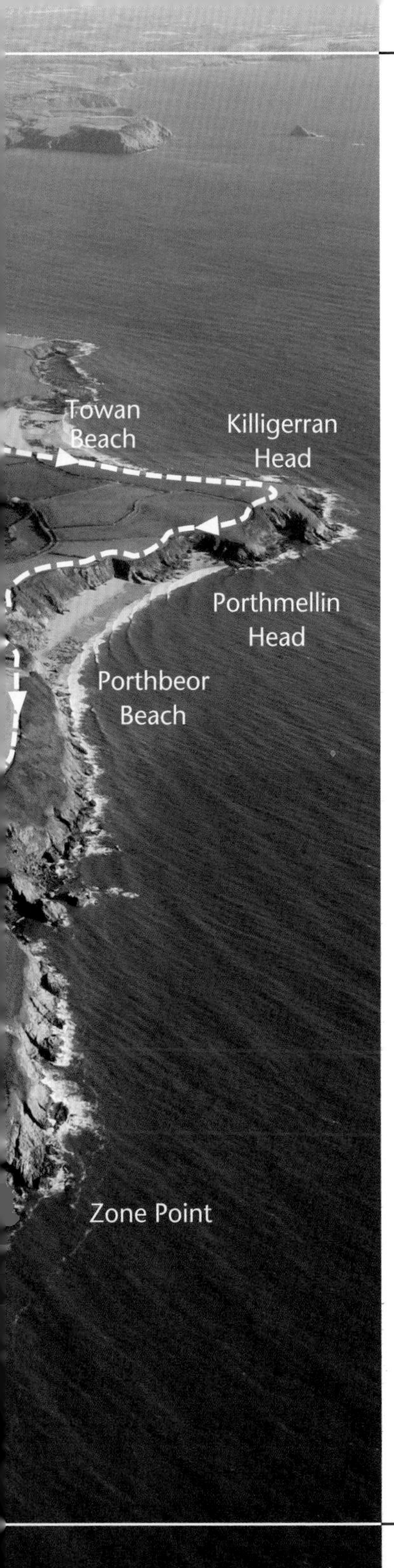

Walk 16 – St Anthony Head

Distance	5.25 miles (8.25km)
Estimated time	2¾ hours
Difficulty	●●●●●
Ascent	756ft (230m)
Map	OS Explorer Map 105
Starting point	SW 867329

Notes: With the wealth of history displayed all around the Roseland peninsula and its spectacular views over Falmouth Bay, as well as Carrick Roads and St Mawes as you turn inland, there are so many features on this walk that you will need to allow plenty of time to assimilate them all. Look out for grey seals and their pups between St Anthony Head and Zone Point.

From the National Trust car park at Porth turn left and take the footpath on your right a few yards beyond, leading to Towan Beach. Turn right onto the South West Coast Path and follow it around the headlands at Killigerran and then Porthmellin. From here it travels above the cliffs at Porthbeor Beach and on around Zone Point and St Anthony Head.

A number of paths snake over Drake's Downs, as you approach Zone Point, and a track leads up to the military road. Stay on the Coast Path, ignoring all these, following it around the viewpoint at St Anthony Head. A detour to the left here will take you to the lighthouse: retrace your steps to the Coast Path if you choose to do this, and carry on around the headland, towards Carricknath Point.

Carry on above St Mawes Harbour and cut across Amsterdam Point to travel above Cellars Beach and go through the woodland beyond to St Anthony Church and Place House. Continue past the church to come out on the road. Turn left here and continue above the Percuil River and into the woods, carrying on ahead when the South West Coast Path stops at the ferry. Stay on this path as it rounds North Hill Point and turns east along Porth Creek and then south to return to the car park at Porth.

St Anthony Head lighthouse.

Carrick Roads, where the rivers Fal and Truro flow together out to sea, is one of Britain's finest deep-water anchorages, and Falmouth Harbour is one of the world's best natural harbours of its kind. Dolphins and porpoises are frequently sighted, and species spotted include the common dolphin, the bottlenose, the Atlantic white-sided, the striped, the white-beaked and Risso's dolphin.

The estuary is also the county's stronghold for two species of diving duck, the Goldeneye and the Red-breasted Merganser. Great Northern and Red-Throated Divers are regular visitors, too, as well as a number of different species of Grebe. There is too much human activity going on to encourage large numbers of wildfowl to the mouth of the rivers; but further inland, especially at Ruan Lanihorne, the mudflats on the creeks attract large numbers of waders, including some of the more rare species such as Wood Sandpipers, and Baird's and Pectoral Sandpipers, as well as some American waders. In the early autumn as many as 30 Spotted Redshanks gather near the hide at Ruan.

Colonies of Fulmars nest on the cliffs at St Anthony Head, and there is a hide for observing them as they glide stiff-winged. Offshore feeding parties of Gannets can be seen, and Shags congregate on a low rock near the lighthouse.

St. Mawes

There is also a wealth of wildlife underwater. Beds of eel grass – Britain's only marine flowering plant – are home to cuttlefish and seahorses, while the calcareous seaweed of the maerl reefs provides shelter for dozens of different plants and animals, including colourful sea slugs and sea anemones.

In 1868, the passing of bye-laws to prohibit oyster-dredging by any mechanically-propelled craft led to the last commercial fleet in Europe to work purely under sail. The gaff cutters of the Port of Truro Oyster Fishery are designed to be able to operate in shallow water, and they use the same methods of harvesting the bivalve molluscs that similar craft have been using for 500 years.

As far back as the Roman times there was a signal station at St Anthony Head, described by archaeologists as a rectangular earthwork some 40 metres square. Through the centuries that followed it was undoubtedly fortified against attack, since the estuary is of such strategic importance, but the first record of artillery here was in 1805, when a battery of 24-pounder guns was sited near the lighthouse. Eighty years later the Stannary Regiment manned new defences on the site where the wartime complex is situated now.

A completely new battery was constructed at the turn of the twentieth century, manned by Falmouth-based 105 Company Royal Garrison Artillery, although in the First World War the Territorial Army took over. When the war ended the guns were removed from the battery and sent away for preservation, while maintenance parties from Pendennis Castle, across the water, kept the battery in a serviceable condition.

When the Second World War broke out the guns were remounted and the Territorials took responsibility again for the defence of the waterway. At the end of the war the Gunners stood down but the battery was kept on standby until 1956, when coast artillery was declared obsolete, following advances in technology as well as the lessons learned on D-Day.

Ramparts at St Anthony Head.

The observation post at St Anthony Head.

Covering 630 miles from Poole to Minehead, the South West Coast Path National Trail leads you through diverse landscapes, all with their own unique story to tell. If the walks in this book have inspired you to find out more about the longest and most popular of the UK's 15 national trails, visit www.southwestcoastpath.com.

Natural England – www.naturalengland.org.uk
Natural England is the government's adviser on the natural environment and provides the majority of the funding for the maintenance of the Coast Path, which is undertaken on a day-to-day basis by Devon County Council and the National Trust. Through Environmental Stewardship Schemes, Natural England also helps farmers and other landowners to protect and enhance the countryside so that nature can thrive.

National Trust – www.nationaltrust.org.uk
The National Trust Countryside Team works seven days a week to restore and care for the characteristic wildlife of the area, as well as working with local communities to improve access and understanding of these special areas. Regular events and opportunities to get involved mean that all ages can help shape their countryside.

South West Coast Path Association – www.southwestcoastpath.org.uk
If you enjoyed these walks, why not join the South West Coast Path Association? This charity represents the users of the trail, campaigns to improve the path and raises money to help it happen. By joining you'll be one of thousands who help to make the South West Coast Path one of the world's greatest walks.

Cornwall Area of Outstanding Natural Beauty – www.cornwall-aonb.gov.uk
The Cornwall AONB makes up approximately a third of the county and is in 12 separate parts. The landscape is diverse and ever changing, cherished by those whose families have worked in it for generations and loved by those who are seeing its beauty and mystery for the first time. It is the essence of Cornwall.

SAFETY

On the beach and coast path

- Stay away from the base of the cliffs and the cliff top and ensure that children and dogs are kept under control.
- Do not climb the cliffs. Rockfalls can happen at any time.
- Beware of mudslides, especially during or after wet weather.
- Always aim to be on the beaches on a falling tide and beware of the incoming tide, especially around headlands. Be sure to check the tide tables.
- Beware of large waves in rough weather, especially on steeply shelving beaches.
- Observe all permanent and temporary warning signs; they advise on hazards and dangers. Check routes beforehand by visiting www.southwestcoastpath.com
- Be very careful on rocky foreshores which often have slippery boulders.
- Stay within your fitness level – some stretches of coast can be strenuous and/or remote.
- Make sure you have the right equipment for the conditions, such as good boots, waterproof clothing and sun screen if appropriate.
- Follow The Countryside Code..

Emergencies

In an emergency dial 999 or 112 and ask for the Coastguard, but be aware that mobile phone coverage in some areas is very limited.